Kids Do,
Animals Too
A Book of Playground Opposites

Debora Pearson • Nora Hilb

Annick Press
Toronto • New York • Vancouver

Annick Press Ltd.

We acknowledge the support of the Canada Council for the Arts, the Ontario Arts Council, and the Government of Canada through the Book Publishing Industry Development Program (BPIDP) for our publishing activities.

Cataloging in Publication

Pearson, Debora
Kids do, animals too : a book of playground opposites /
by Debora Pearson ; art by Nora Hilb.

ISBN 1-55037-923-2 (bound).—ISBN 1-55037-922-4 (pbk.)

1. English language—Synonyms and antonyms—Juvenile literature.
I. Hilb, Nora   II. Title.

PE1591.P42 2005   j428.1   C2005-901571-3

The art in this book was rendered in watercolor.
The text was typeset in Myriad Condensed.

Distributed in Canada by:
Firefly Books Ltd.
66 Leek Crescent
Richmond Hill, ON
L4B 1H1

Published in the U.S.A. by:
Annick Press (U.S.) Ltd.
Distributed in the U.S.A. by:
Firefly Books (U.S.) Inc.
P.O. Box 1338
Ellicott Station
Buffalo, NY 14205

Printed in China.

Visit us at: www.annickpress.com

For Chloe and Madeline Carmichael, two special girls
—D.P.

For my Mum, with joy and love
—N.H.

fast

Katie and her puppy race to the park.

slow

Tom and his dog roll s-l-o-w-l-y there.

in

Jillian is in the stroller.
Noah is out.

out

A family of mice curl up in their nest.
Two mice scramble out.

up

Sam goes up.
Hiroko zips down.

down

One squirrel hurries up a tree.
One skitters all the way down.

on

Ella sits on a swing.
Karim jumps off.

One toad rests on a bumpy log.
One springs off – Boing! Ka-flop!

ahead

Max is ahead of Lily.
Lily is behind Max.

behind

Ants rush by. A big one is ahead.
A small ant scampers after it.

quiet

Daddy is quiet.
Simon is loud.

loud

A mother bird is silent as
she feeds her chirping birds.

under

**Theo hides under a blanket.
Asha crawls over it.**

over

One spider runs under some leaves.
One roams over them.

wet

Splish-splash! Rosa is wet.
Peter stays dry in the sand.

dry

One duck takes a cool, quick bath.
Its mate waits on the grass.

toward

Jack dashes toward Martin.
Molly tiptoes away.

away

**Butterflies flit toward flowers.
One zigzags away.**

asleep

Tired Katie falls asleep.
Tom stays awake.

awake

Squirrels curl up and close their eyes . . .

Bats wake up and play.